WORLD CRAFTS

TOYS

Meryl Doney

FRANKLIN WATTS
A Division of Grolier Publishing
New York • London • Sydney • Hong Kong
Danbury, Connecticut

About this book

So many different toys are enjoyed by children around the world that it would take several books to cover all of them. Here we have chosen a few toys from a variety of countries to give you an idea of the wide range.

This book begins with simple toys made out of natural objects, like the painted stones from Haiti. It goes on to look at some of the ingenious moving toys made by children in Mexico, India, and South America. No one can write about toys without mentioning dolls, and we have a section that draws on the thousands available. Bicycles, cars, trucks, and airplanes are among the many transportation toys that are made and enjoyed by their owners. And finally, there is the wonderful world of kites, which brings people outdoors.

Most of the steps given to make the toys are very easy to follow, but where you see this sign ask for help from an adult.

Children often use the simple materials around them to make their toys. They are very skillful at recycling things. The wire plane from Zimbabwe and the bottle-top snake from Mexico are good examples. See what you can invent with the objects around you, such as natural materials, household goods, or discarded packaging.

A toy collection

If you enjoy making the toys in this book, you might like to start a toy collection. Explore craft and toy stores, charity shops, and cultural centers to see what you can find. And, of course, if relatives or friends go abroad, they may be able to bring back an unusual toy for you. You could begin collecting toys from one country or start a collection of one type of toy, for example, dolls or *tap taps* (see page 24). Learn more about your toy collection by finding books on the history of toys from different countries at your local library.

First published in the United States in 1995 by Franklin Watts
Text © 1995 by Meryl Doney

Franklin Watts
95 Madison Avenue
New York, NY 10016

10 9 8 7 6 5 4 3 2 1

Series editor: Annabel Martin
Editor: Jane Walker
Design: Visual Image
Cover design: Mike Davis
Artwork: Ruth Levy
Photography: Peter Millard

With special thanks to Alison Croft, educational advisor and toy maker.

Library of Congress Cataloging-in-Publication Data:

Doney, Meryl, 1942 –
    Toys/by Meryl Doney.
      p.   cm. – (World Crafts)
    Includes index.
    ISBN 0-531-14400-3
    1. Toy making – Juvenile literature.
    [1. Toy making.] I. Title. II. Series.
    TT174.D66 1995   95-10735
    745.592–dc20   CIP AC

Printed in Great Britain

Contents

The world of toys

Toys must have been around for as long as there have been children to play with them. Bone whistles and fragments of small clay figures that may have been used as toys have been found. Some date back to the Stone Age.

More definite evidence has been found in China, dating from around 5000 B.C., and in India and ancient Egypt. In Thebes, on Egypt's Nile river, pull-along crocodiles, leopards, and jointed dolls were buried in tombs. By the time of the Greek and Roman civilizations, toys were well known.

Since these early times, toys have continued to be developed all over the world, because children love to play. Some toys have a double function, such as the African dolls that are given as toys but are also meant to act as powerful charms to ward off evil. Toys also help to prepare children for the adult world. In Indonesia, as soon as a baby smiles he or she is given gifts: a miniature wooden shield, sword, and spear for a boy, a fireplace and cooking equipment for a girl.

During the eighteenth century, European reformers, such as Friedrich Fröbel, began to realize the educational value of toys such as bricks, puzzles, and games. From then on, toys became an important part of school life.

Today, most children's toys are manufactured and sold all over the world. But there is also great interest in traditional toys. We hope you will enjoy inventing your own toys, using some of these techniques, as well as sharing them with your friends.

Your own toy-making kit

As you begin making your toys, look around for odd bits of material, buttons, cardboard tubes, and yogurt containers. Keep these items and a set of tools in a box ready to use when you want to make a toy.

Make some dough from the recipe below and store that, too. Cover it with plastic wrap, and keep it in a container with a tight lid.

Here are some of the most useful items for your toy-making kit:

hammer • small saw • hacksaw • large nail or awl • hand drill • needle-nose pliers • scissors • craft knife • metal ruler • brushes • gesso • poster paints • varnish • white household glue • tube of strong glue • plastic modeling material • modeling clay • clear tape • masking tape • oaktag • paper •

tissue paper • newspaper • pen • pencil • felt pens • fabric and felt • needle and thread • decorations, including sequins, braid, tin foil, stickers, and beads • newspaper and cardboard to work on • apron • paper towels for cleaning up

Potato dough

This dough recipe comes from Peru. It is made from mashed potatoes and plaster of Paris.

3 tablespoons of instant mashed potato
10 tablespoons of plaster of Paris
water

In a small bowl, mix the mashed potato with 4 fluid ounces (150 ml) of boiling water. Beat with a fork until water is absorbed.

In a larger bowl, mix the plaster with 3 tablespoons of cold water. Stir with a spoon until smooth.

Add the potato to the plaster and mix well. Form into a dough and knead well.

No cooking is required for this dough.

Papier mâché

Papier mâché means chewed paper! But don't worry, this method only involves building up many layers of glued paper over an existing object or model.

Cover the object you wish to copy with petroleum jelly (like Vaseline) to stop the paper from sticking to it.

Mix one tablespoon of white glue with a little water in a bowl. Tear a sheet of newspaper into small squares. Dip a paintbrush in the glue and pick up a square with it. Lay it in place on the model and paint some glue over it.

Add more and more squares in this way until the whole model is covered.

Repeat this process several times. Leave in a warm, airy place to dry.

Simple toys

Catching a ball may well have been the very first game played by children. In Egyptian tomb paintings and carvings, on Greek vases, and on Roman murals there are pictures of balls being thrown. The balls were made from wood, rubber, or feathers bound with leather. Some were sewn from rags, wound from strands of wool or cotton, or even formed of compressed cow dung. The bamboo ball above was made in Thailand, and the crocheted cotton one (right) has the colors of South Africa.

Figures and creatures that are made from natural objects are equally easy to make and play with. These brightly painted stones come from Haiti in the Caribbean. The pebbles have been collected from the beach and painted to look somewhat like fish.

Maybe the shape of a stick gave a South African child the idea for the curvy snake. It is simply whittled with a craft knife and painted.

Make painted stone creatures

Find a stone or pebble that has an unusual shape. If you are visiting the beach, a pebble will be ideal. Look at it from all angles and see if its shape suggests a person's face, or perhaps an animal, bird, or fish. If you paint the stone white first, it will be easier to see its shape clearly.

You will need: stone or pebble · gesso · pencil · paints · felt pen · varnish · paper · glue · materials for decoration: oaktag, clay, dough, papier mâché, sequins, beads, colored paper, string, wool, fabric, raffia

1 Paint your stone with gesso.

2 Draw in pencil the shapes you want on your stone. Fill in the shapes by painting areas of color. Keep your design simple and bold.

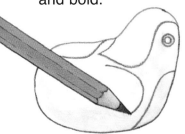

3 When the paint is dry, neaten the edges by going over the original pencil lines with a felt pen. Add a coat of varnish.

4 The brightly colored bird has a paper beak. Roll a piece of paper into a cone shape. Use strong glue to attach it to the stone.

5 You could add any number of extra features to your creature, like wings, a tail, scales, fins, ears, or a nose. Use materials such as beads, string, wool, and raffia.

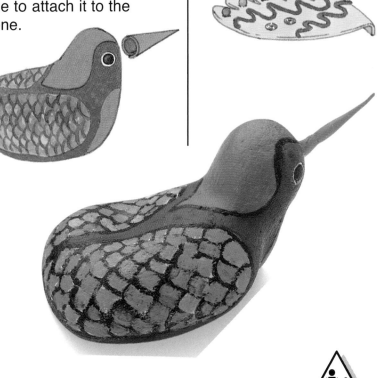

You could make a snake, lizard, or crocodile from an interestingly shaped stick. Choose a piece of old dry wood. Strip off the bark, and make the stick into a rough shape with a penknife. Add details, and paint as above.

Toys with bobbing heads

Toys with bobbing heads are produced in many different areas of the world. They are made by finding an object's perfect balancing point. The tortoise was made from a walnut shell in the Indian state of Bihar. Its legs are pieces of wood from an old packing case. The carved wooden head and tail are suspended by wire loops so they can nod and wave when you touch them.

The same principle was used to make the colorful little aardvark from India. His body is a small seed pod, and his tail is the pod's stalk. The head and legs are twigs, but the aardvark's ears are little pieces of red plastic.

Make Aard the Vark

1 With a pencil, mark four points for legs, $\frac{1}{2}$ in (1.5 cm) apart, on either side of the Ping-Pong ball seam. Draw a circle, $\frac{1}{2}$ in (1.5 cm) in diameter, for the head hole as shown. Mark a point on the bottom of the ball for the tail.

2 To cut out the head hole, carefully pierce with a pin and then use small pointed scissors. Pierce holes in all the other marks. Insert used matches to form four legs and a tail. Glue in place, making sure Aard stands up firmly.

3 With a craft knife, remove bark and sharpen the end of the twig. (Always work away from yourself.) Paint on nose and eyes. Paint body and legs. Cut two tiny ear shapes from cardboard or heavy plastic. Glue in position.

4 Tie thread around middle of twig and hold it up. Move knot along until the head balances perfectly. Glue in place.

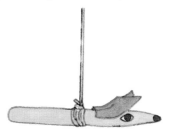

5 Thread needle and push it in through the head hole and out through the top of the ball. When the head balances in the center of hole, glue thread in position on top of the body. Cut off extra thread.

Slithery snakes

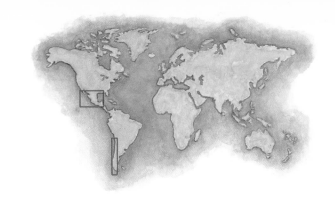

Snakes make great toys, probably because of the way they move, and they are so easy to make.

Ruperto Monsalve runs a workshop in Villarrica, southern Chile, where he makes slithery crocodiles and snakes like the one shown below. The secret of their lifelike movements is a strip of leather. It is glued along the length of the snake between the two halves.

The snake on the left is from Mexico. It has been made from metal bottle tops and corks. The face is painted to look menacing. The string that threads through its body sticks out of the mouth like a tongue.

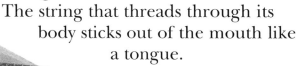

Make a bottle-top snake

You will need: 100 metal bottle tops • plastic modeling material • large nail or awl • hammer • champagne cork • wine cork • craft knife • large needle • green garden string • felt pens

You will need about 100 bottle tops to make a good long snake. You could collect them from friends or at school. You might know someone who works in a bar serving drinks from bottles. Give that person a large plastic container with a lid and ask if the tops could be collected for you.

1 Place each bottle top, in turn, upside down on the plastic modeling material. Make a hole in each top by placing the nail or awl in the center and giving it a sharp tap with a hammer.

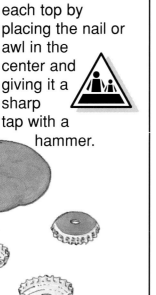

2 With a craft knife, shape the champagne cork into the snake's head.

Cut out a wedge-shaped mouth. Taper the wine cork so that it looks like the end of the snake's tail.

3 Thread the string through the eye of a large needle. Using the needle, thread the string through the mouth, each bottle top, and finally the cork tail.

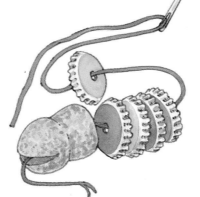

4 Knot the string at both ends. Leave it hanging out of the mouth to form the tongue. Decorate the face and tail with felt pens.

Wriggling toys

All over India, toy sellers can be seen offering a dazzling selection of brightly decorated toys. Many are made from the simplest of materials. As well as these toys that are made to sell, the ones that Indian children make for themselves are also very inventive. Children there use leaves, seeds, paper, cotton, and anything else that comes to hand.

These toys from India are very simple to make from scraps, yet their mechanisms are quite sophisticated.

When the toy on the right is turned over, the four birds (or are they fish?) wriggle down the threads as though they were alive. Reverse the toy and off they go again.

The snake is driven by a rubber band and a small clay drum, such as an empty spool of thread. One pull on the string is enough to start the snake wiggling along the ground to frighten nervous relatives.

Make a wriggly snake

1 Model the clay into a roller in the shape of a spool. Using a large needle, make two holes lengthwise through the roller. Leave clay to harden.

You will need: a small piece of self-hardening clay (the size of a small spool of thread) • needle • scissors • oaktag, approx. 4 x 6 in (9 x 14 cm) • flexible wire • pliers • thin elastic • string • a long strip of computer paper • glue • ribbon • paints

2 Cut oaktag into a head shape. Make two holes in both sides. Thread the wire through the holes, bending it to form a domed shape. Using pliers, twist the ends of the wire into hook shapes.

3 Cut the elastic band. Wind string around the roller and thread through the head with the needle. Using the needle, thread the elastic band through one wire hook, one hole in the spool, the second hook, and the second hole. Knot the elastic in place.

4 Cut out a strip of computer paper, 3 x 21$\frac{1}{2}$ in (80 x 550 mm). Taper one end as shown. Fold paper in half lengthwise, then into a small accordian.

5 With the folded side toward you, gently push each accordian point inward, by $\frac{1}{4}$ in (5 mm), on alternate sides to form triangle shapes.

6 Open all the triangles and flatten the paper. Refold it along the zigzag lines (marked in red) to form a bent accordian.

7 Trim neck and glue to head. Add a ribbon tongue and tail. Paint and decorate.

Miniature world

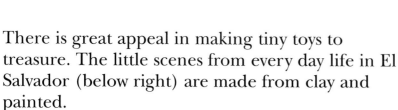

There is great appeal in making tiny toys to treasure. The little scenes from every day life in El Salvador (below right) are made from clay and painted.

The small woven basket has been made by hand in Ecuador. The brooch beside it is in the shape of a llama that is decorated with flowers.

The hair barrette below is decorated with Guatemalan worry dolls. Guatemalan children keep these tiny dolls in a special box. Each one is a different character. The children tell one of their worries to each doll, and then hide the dolls under their pillow at night. By the morning the dolls have taken all their worries away!

Make a box of worry dolls

The recipe on page 5 for uncooked potato dough is ideal for making your own miniatures or brooches. You could copy the ones shown opposite, or make scenes showing what life is like where you live.

1 Cut a matchstick in half. Wrap and glue light cardboard around one end of the match to form a face. Draw on the face with felt pens. Wrap and glue fabric around the rest of the match to form the skirt.

2 To make arms, wrap yarn tightly around a length of wire. Glue in place. Cut off a 1-in (3-cm) piece for the arms. Glue to the doll's back.

3 Wrap yarn diagonally several times across the upper body. Repeat the other way to secure the arms. Glue the end at the back.

Repeat this method to make as many more dolls as you want. Use different colored fabrics and yarns for the dolls.

4 Make a home for your dolls by decorating a matchbox with paint or fabric, and adding a button or tassel as a pull. Line the box with a scrap of fabric.

These dolls have a matchbox home, but you can also use them as decorations. Glue them to an old hair barrette. Or make a brooch by sticking the dolls onto a strip of cardboard and sewing a safety pin onto the back.

Peg doll and apple granny

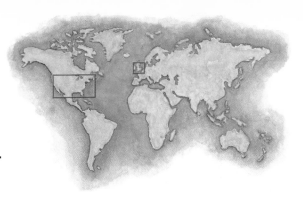

Wooden dolls have been made all over Europe since earliest times. The most famous toy makers were those from Seiffen in Saxony, Germany, where wood carvers have been at work since the Middle Ages.

The simple wooden doll below was probably made in England, where the London-based toy-making industry began to develop after 1880. Later, dolls like her were made from hardwood clothes pegs and known as peg dolls.

The Pioneers who moved westwards across North America in the nineteenth century made dolls for their children. This unusual doll (left), called an apple granny, began as a young woman and then aged to become a grandmother within a few weeks. The secret of this magic is in the apple, which shrinks and makes the wrinkles on granny's face.

Make a doll from an apple

You can make a simple clothespin doll using a hardwood clothespin. Paint a face on the clothespin. Wind and glue a pipe cleaner around the body to form arms. Make clothes from felt scraps.

Choose a large apple to make your apple granny; you will be surprised how much it shrinks in a few weeks.

You will need: a large apple • paring knife • 3 tsp salt • bowl • cork • stiff cardboard circle, 2³/₄ in (7 cm) in diameter • white glue • chopstick • scissors • 3¹/₂-in (9-cm) strip of oaktag • scraps of flesh-colored felt • needle and thread • dress fabric, 5¹/₂ x 13¹/₂ in (14 x 34 cm) • scraps of fabric, ribbon, and lace • wool yarn • fabric circle, 4 in (11 cm) in diameter • two beads • 4 in (11 cm) of fuse wire

1 Peel apple. Use a vegetable knife to carve out the face. (Remember to cut away from your body.) Put apple in a small bowl, add salt and water to cover. Leave overnight.

2 Glue cork to center of cardboard circle. Make a hole in the cork and glue in the chopstick. When dry, push apple onto chopstick. Leave in warm, dry place for a few days.

3 Cut arms from the strip of oaktag. Stick felt on each side and trim to shape. Glue arms to chopstick. Bind scraps of cloth around the body and sew in place.

4 Fold dress fabric in half and cut a T shape. Cut hole for head. Sew up the sides (leaving armholes open) and hem. Put dress on doll, fold over and glue the neck edges. Make apron from a scrap of lace or cloth. Sew an 11-in (28-cm) ribbon across top.

5 Stick on wool yarn for hair. To make hat, sew lace around edge of the fabric circle. Sew a circle of large stitches ³/₄ in (2 cm) from the edge. Pull this tight to gather up the fabric. Tie the ends of the thread.

6 Stick a bead into each eyehole. To make glasses, loop wire twice around a pencil. Push ends of wire into sides of doll's head.

Nesting dolls

These nested dolls are traditionally called *Matryoshka* dolls. Today they are the best-known Russian dolls and are made all over Russia and the former Soviet Union. Surprisingly, however, the idea for small wooden figures that fit neatly into one another originally came from Japan. In the late nineteenth century the little figure of Daruma the Sage was brought from Japan to the Gorky region of Russia. A Russian artist, Sergei Malyutin, and a wood carver, Vladivere Zvezdochkin, transformed the figure into a set of Russian characters: six girls, one boy and a baby.

This set was made in Belarus. The dolls are dressed in traditional costume and decorated with a large, red flower. Red is a popular color in Russia. It symbolizes the rising and setting sun, and is the color of strength and life.

Make five dolls in one

1 Form a doll shape 1 in (2.5 cm) tall from plastic modeling material. Give it a flat base so that it stands firmly. Cover with several layers of papier mâché and leave to dry.

2 Roll out a thin layer of modeling material. Wrap it around first doll and form into a second doll shape. Add one layer of wet tissue paper. (This prevents your finished doll from sticking to the modeling material.) Add several layers of papier mâché and leave to dry.

3 Use a craft knife to cut through the outer layer of papier mâché at the widest point around the middle. Slip the two halves off the modeling material.

If this is difficult, dig out some of the modeling material with a penknife blade.

4 Remove thin layer of modeling material to reveal the first (smallest) doll.

5 Glue a strip of light oaktag around the inside of the bottom half of the second doll, to form a lip. Replace the top half. Repeat this process with a second doll to make a third and so on. Make the dolls bigger each time.

6 Paint each doll with gesso. Decorate and varnish.

Wooden horses

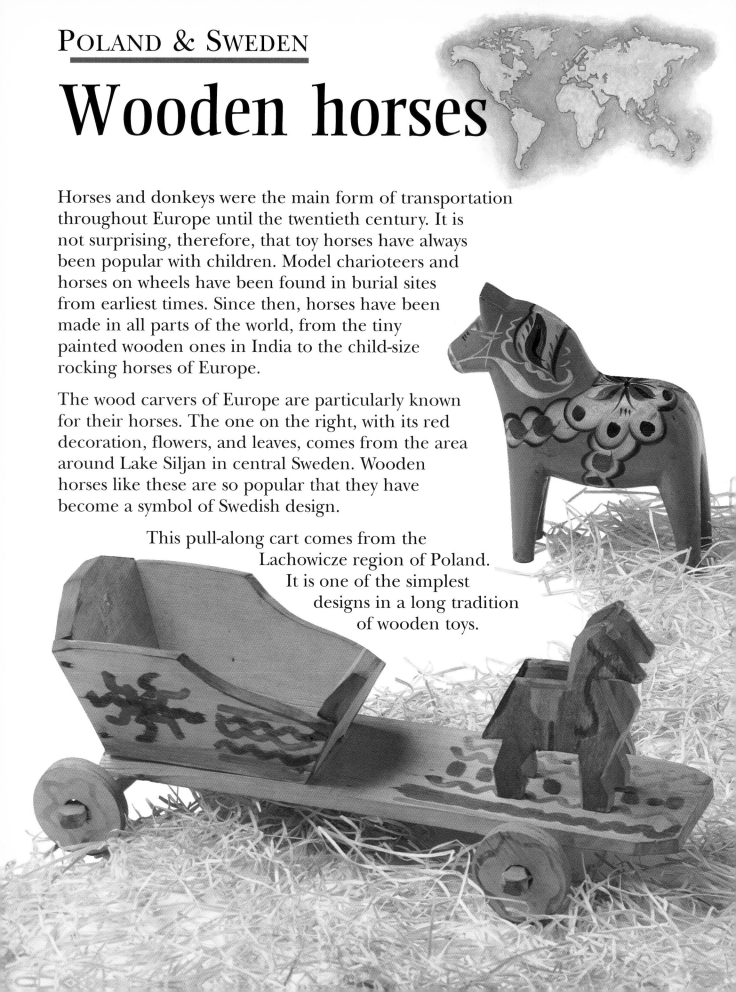

Horses and donkeys were the main form of transportation throughout Europe until the twentieth century. It is not surprising, therefore, that toy horses have always been popular with children. Model charioteers and horses on wheels have been found in burial sites from earliest times. Since then, horses have been made in all parts of the world, from the tiny painted wooden ones in India to the child-size rocking horses of Europe.

The wood carvers of Europe are particularly known for their horses. The one on the right, with its red decoration, flowers, and leaves, comes from the area around Lake Siljan in central Sweden. Wooden horses like these are so popular that they have become a symbol of Swedish design.

This pull-along cart comes from the Lachowicze region of Poland. It is one of the simplest designs in a long tradition of wooden toys.

Make a horse-drawn cart

This toy is made with stiff cardboard and so it is not very strong. If you are good at woodwork, you could use the same pattern to make a much stronger cart from plywood.

You will need: a piece of graph paper · pencil and ruler · thick corrugated cardboard · clear tape · craft knife · metal ruler · strong glue · $\frac{1}{2}$-in (1.5-cm) dowel · awl · four $\frac{3}{4}$-in (2-cm) screws · gesso · poster paints · varnish · vise

1 On graph paper, draw out patterns for cart as shown.

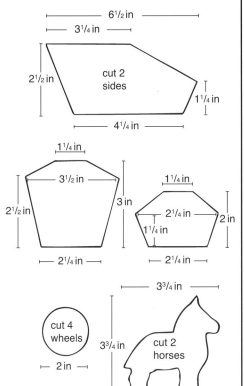

6½ in
3¼ in
cut 2 sides
2½ in
1¼ in
4¼ in

1¼ in
3½ in
2½ in
3 in
1¼ in
2¼ in
2 in
1¼ in
2¼ in
2¼ in

cut 4 wheels
2 in
3¾ in
3¾ in
cut 2 horses

2 Attach paper to the cardboard with tape. Using a craft knife and metal ruler, cut out all pieces plus a rectangle, 12 x 3.5 in (30 x 9 cm), for base. Cut off corners at one end of base.

3 Stick the front and back pieces between the two sides with strong glue. Glue cart and horses to base.

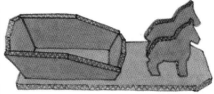

4 Cut two pieces of $\frac{1}{2}$-in (1.5-cm) dowel 4 in (11 cm) long. Mark at $\frac{1}{2}$ in (1 cm) in from each end. Grip dowel in vise. With craft knife, cut into dowel at both marks. Carve out wood between marks to form flat surface. Repeat with second dowel.

5 Make a hole in the end of each dowel with an awl. Use a screwdriver to push a $\frac{3}{4}$-in (2-cm) screw through each wheel and into the end of the dowels.

6 Paint the whole cart with gesso and then decorate with poster paints. Varnish.

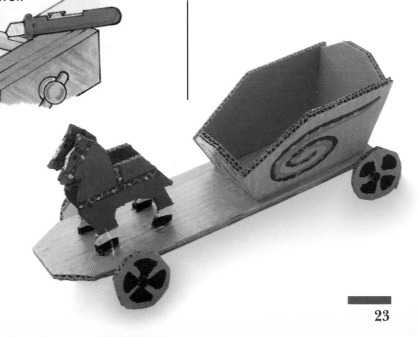

Brightly colored transportation

The tiny country of Haiti has no organized public transportation, so a system of privately owned trucks has developed. They are called *tap taps* (shown right), and are their owner's pride and joy. *Tap taps* are often painted in bright colors and decorated with Bible texts, prayers, or slogans. Passengers are crammed inside and their luggage, produce, and livestock are piled on top.

The same means of transportation is popular in the villages of South America. There the open-sided wooden trucks are called *chivas*. Their decorations often depict wedding parties, religious processions, or funerals. Pottery workers in the villages of Ecuador and Colombia make these children's toy *chivas* (below right).

The tin truck (below center) comes from Senegal in West Africa, and the wooden *"A" Team* truck (below left) from South Africa.

Make your own truck

Look closely at the trucks and vans on the facing page. They are made from papier mâché, clay, tin, and wood. We have given instructions for making the wooden *"A" Team* truck, but you may like to try your hand at making copies of the others, or inventing your own form of transportation toy.

You will need: two pieces of wood, $3/4$ x $1^3/4$ x $18^1/2$ in (2 x 4.5 x 46 cm), and $1/2$ x $2^3/4$ x 14 in (1.5 x 7 x 35 cm) • sandpaper • hammer • sixteen $3/4$-in (2-cm) nails • $3/4$-in (2-cm) quarter-dowel, $2^1/2$ in (6 cm) long • a length of $1^1/2$ in (4-cm) dowel • hand drill • gesso • poster paints • varnish • four washers • four $1^1/2$-in (3.5-cm) screws • wood glue • vise

1 Mark the wood into four $2^3/4$-in (7-cm) and three $2^1/4$-in (6-cm) lengths.

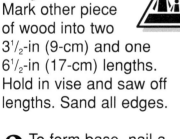

Mark other piece of wood into two $3^1/2$-in (9-cm) and one $6^1/2$-in (17-cm) lengths. Hold in vise and saw off lengths. Sand all edges.

2 To form base, nail a $2^3/4$-in (7-cm) piece of wood to each end of the $6^1/2$-in (17-cm) base.

3 To form truck body, nail two $2^3/4$-in (7-cm) pieces to a $3^1/2$-in (9-cm) piece. Turn over and nail the other $3^1/2$-in (9-cm) piece onto the ends, forming a box.

4 To form cab, stack two $2^1/2$-in (6-cm) pieces of wood on top of each other and nail together. Turn over, add the third $2^1/2$-in (6-cm) piece and nail. Nail the quarter-dowel to the top of the stack.

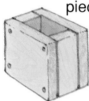

5 To make the wheels, hold the $1^1/2$-in (4-cm) dowel in the vise. Saw four $1/2$-in (1.5-cm) pieces off the end. Pencil a mark in center of each wheel, hold in vise, and drill a hole.

6 Paint all pieces with gesso and poster paint. Varnish. When dry, screw each wheel to base, with washers in between. Glue cab and back onto base.

Airplanes and bicycles

Here are some more examples of ingenious toys. These were made from wire in Zimbabwe. The airplane was made by two craftsmen, Enock and Bernard, who have been making wire toys since they were young boys. They now export their toys all over the world.

When the boy on the bicycle is pushed along the ground, his arms beat out a rhythm on the shoe polish lid. He is dressed in clothes sewn from scraps of cloth and his hat is a lid from an oil bottle.

The shaped wheel axle is a clever way to make parts of the model move up and down. The mechanism is a little tricky to master. However, when you have successfully made the bicycle drummer, you may like to go on to design your own wire toy with moving parts.

Make a bicycle drummer

1 Untwist a coat hanger with pliers and straighten. Bend one end in a circle inside the tin lid. Bend the next 4 in (10 cm) to form a support for the drum. Hold with pliers and bend to form a complete circle 2³/₄ in (7 cm) in diameter.

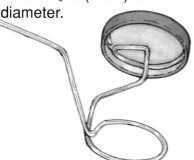

Bend the wire upward to make a seat for the drummer, and finally backward to form the handle.

2 Snip the hook from the second coat hanger and straighten. Form the wheels and shaped axle from this wire. Make sure the wheels are bigger than the axle shapes so that the axles do not hit the ground.

3 With 13 feet (4 m) of flexible wire form the body and neck. Leave twisted ends at back. Form arms using 9-foot (2.8-m) pieces. Twist ends around a pencil several times to make drumsticks. Make loops at elbows and ends, and bend at shoulders.

4 Make two arm-movers from 4-foot (1.3-m) pieces. Loop at both ends. Form legs from 11-foot (3.6-m) piece of wire.

5 To make head, stuff pieces of tights into toe of one leg. Push wire neck into head. Sew neck tightly. Twist rest of tights leg around body. Push arms through shoulder loops and close end loops. Push legs through hip loops.

6 Dress your drummer from scraps of material. Add a bottle top for a hat.

7 To assemble, twist end of body wire around "seat" and ends of legs around bottom circle. Wind florist's wire around bottom circle and under axle at both sides to hold in place. Leave axle free to turn. Loop arm movers through elbows and around shapes, fixing in place with more florist's wire.

Toys to catch the wind

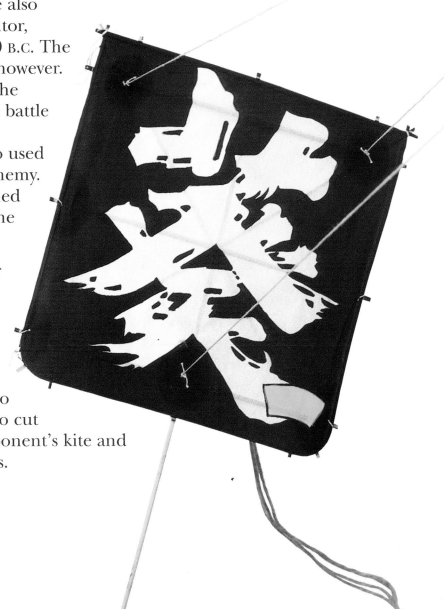

All over the world toys have been invented to catch the power of the wind. Paper kites on a bamboo frame may have originated in China about 3,000 years ago, although there are also records of a Greek kite inventor, Archytas of Tarentum, in 400 B.C. The Chinese kites were not toys, however. They were used to measure the distance between armies in a battle or to carry a rope across a dangerous river. Soldiers also used whistling kites to scare the enemy. They were fitted with tightened strings that wailed eerily in the wind.

Today kite flying is a popular sport in Japan. Annual festivals are held involving battles between enormous kites that are flown by whole teams of flyers. Powdered glass is dusted onto the kite's string. The aim is to cut through the string of an opponent's kite and capture the kite where it falls.

Make a mini kite

1 Lay a stick on folded newspaper. With a craft knife, whittle off the top layer, leaving a flat surface. Turn the stick over and do the same to the other side. Repeat with the other sticks. Shorten one stick to 7½ in (19 cm).

You will need: five green 12-in (30-cm) bamboo garden sticks • newspaper • craft knife • construction paper • poster paints • large brush • white glue mixed with a little water • strong glue • cotton yarn • silk thread • needle • string • very long length of nylon thread (or a prepared spool from a kite shop)

2 Cut a piece of construction paper, 8 x 9½ in (19.5 x 24.5 cm). Fold in edges by ½ in (1 cm) all around and then open again. Paint a design on the front with poster paints and leave to dry.

3 Paint glue mixture all over the back. Add a dot of strong glue at each corner.

4 Lay the five sticks across the sticky surface as shown. Fold paper edges back over the stick ends and press firmly. Tie the sticks at center and at top corners with cotton yarn.

5 Paint glue mixture over the decorated front. As it dries, the paper will become taut like a drum.

6 Thread a needle with silk thread. On the front of the kite, pierce paper at top right-hand corner and tie end of silk firmly around bamboo sticks. Repeat on left, forming a loop 17 in (44 cm) long. Attach a third silk strand to the middle stick, 2¾ in (7 cm) from bottom. Tie the other end to the top of the loop, forming a triangle.

7 Cut three 40-in (100-cm) lengths of string and tie at one end. Attach this tail with silk to the center back of the kite. To fly your kite, attach nylon thread to the triangle of silk thread.

Get together with a group of friends, your class at school, or a youth group, and try to make a really big kite to fly as a team. You will need to find a book on kite making, and a big, windy space in which to try out your creation.

Useful information

Equipment and materials

Most supplies are available in local craft and hobby stores, and even five-and-ten cent stores. The Yellow Pages will have many of the places listed, and you can find the ones closest to you. Here are some that can be contacted.

Leisurecrafts Inc.
3061 Maria Street
Compton, CA 90224
(213) 537-5150

Pearl Paint Co.
1033 E. Oakland Park Boulevard
Ft. Lauderdale, FL 33334
(305) 564-5700

Trost Model & Craft
3129 W. 47th Street
Chicago, IL 60632
(312) 927-1400

The Brighten-Up Shop
618 Central Avenue
Great Falls, MT 59401
(406) 453-8273

S & R Distributing Co.
714 Greenville Boulevard
Greenville, NC 27834
(919) 756-9565

A Hobby Hut
2835 Nostrand Avenue
Brooklyn, NY 11229
(718) 338-2554

Pearl Paint Co.
308 Canal Street
New York, NY 10013
(212) 431-7932

Dupey Management Corp.
P.O. Box 169029
Irving, TX 75063
(214) 929-8595

Thomas Wholesale
5641D General Washington
Drive
Alexandria, VA 22312
(703) 820-9790

Craf-T Inc.
P.O. Box 44577
Tacoma, WA 98444
(206) 537-5353

Tri-County Distributors
2785 S. 167th Street
New Berlin, WI 53151
(414) 782-2120

Museums

Museums often have items for sale in a gift shop. You can also try thrift shops or second-hand stores for used toys and dolls and even fabrics and tools.

The Doll House Museum
201 Church Street
Blackstone, VA 23824
(804) 292-3487

Dollhouse Museum of the
Southwest
2208 Routh Street
Dallas, TX 75201
(214) 969-5502

Eliza Cruce Hall Doll Museum
320 "E" Northwest
Ardmore, OK 73401
(405) 223-8290

Eugene Field House and
Toy Museum
634 S. Broadway
St. Louis, MO 63102
(314) 421-4689

House Of A Thousand Dolls
106 First Street
Loma, MT 59460
(406) 739-4338

Pauline E. Glidden Toy Museum
Pleasant Street
Ashland, NH 03217
(603) 968-7289

San Francisco International
Toy Museum
The Cannery
2801 Leavenworth Street
San Francisco, CA 94133
(415) 441-8697

Toy and Miniature Museum of
Kansas City
5235 Oak Street
Kansas City, MO 64112
(816) 333-2055

Washington Dolls' House and
Toy Museum
5236 44th Street NW
Chevy Chase,
Washington, D.C. 20015
(202) 244-0024

Yesteryears Doll and Toy
Museum
Main and River Streets
Sandwich, MA 02563
(508) 888-1711

Books

Eden Toys Staff.
Toys and Designs from the World of Beatrix Potter.
New York: Warne, 1992.

Flick, Pauline.
Discovering Toys and Toy Museums.
Hatboro, PA:
Legacy Books, 1977.

Hutchings, Margaret.
Big Book of Stuffed Toys and Doll Making.
New York: Dover, 1983.

Jaffke, Freya.
Toymaking with Children.
Beltsville, MA:
Gryphon House, 1988.

Lemke, Stefan and Marie-Luise L. Pricker.
Making Toys and Gifts.
Chicago: Childrens Press, 1991.

Lohf, Sabine.
Building Your Own Toys.
Chicago: Childrens Press, 1989.

Werner, Vivian.
Dolls. New York: Avon, 1991.

Young, Robert S.
Dolls. New York: Dillon, 1992.

Glossary

apprentice Someone who learns a skill from an expert.

balsa Very soft, light wood from the balsa tree.

burial site A place where many people have been buried.

charioteer A person who drove a horse-drawn racing cart called a chariot.

charm An object that is believed to have magic powers.

crochet A method of making fabric by looping wool or cotton with a hook.

fragment A small piece that has broken off something.

livestock Live animals that are kept for their milk, wool, or meat.

***Matyroshka* doll** A traditional painted wooden doll from the former Soviet Union. Each doll is hollow and fits inside another one.

Mesolithic A period of ancient history that was part of the Stone Age.

Mesopotamia An ancient kingdom on the site of modern Iraq.

Middle Ages A period of history between A.D. 1000 and 1400.

mural A picture that is painted directly onto a wall.

pioneer One of the people who traveled westward across North America to start up new settlements and towns.

pre-Columbian A period in South American history before the continent was discovered by the explorer Christopher Columbus.

raffia Fiber from the palm tree. It is used to tie plants and make hats and baskets.

replica A copy.

sage A wise person.

tap tap A truck that is used to transport people and their luggage in Haiti.

whittle To carve with a knife.

worry doll A tiny doll from Guatemala. Children believe that worry dolls will take away their worries.

Index

Additional photographs:

page 10 (top): James Merrell, from *Living with Folk Art* by Nicholas Barnard, published by Thames and Hudson, London, 1991.